EARLY SCIENCE

NONLIVING THING

KIM THOMPSON

A Crabtree Roots Book

Crabtree Publishing
crabtreebooks.com

School-to-Home Support for Caregivers and Teachers

This book helps children grow by letting them practice reading. Here are a few guiding questions to help the reader with building his or her comprehension skills. Possible answers appear here in red.

Before Reading:

• What do I think this book is about?
  - *I think this book is about objects found in the world.*
  - *I think this book is about things that are not alive.*

• What do I want to learn about this topic?
  - *I want to learn how to tell if something is living or not.*
  - *I want to learn what things around me are not living.*

During Reading:

• I wonder why...
  - *I wonder if plants can move.*
  - *I wonder if robots are alive.*

• What have I learned so far?
  - *I have learned that nonliving things do not need food or water.*
  - *I have learned that nonliving things do not grow.*

After Reading:

• What details did I learn about this topic?
  - *I have learned that nonliving things do not move on their own.*
  - *I have learned that nonliving things do not breathe.*

• Read the book again and look for the vocabulary words.
  - *I see the word **drink** on page 4 and the word **breathe** on page 6. The other vocabulary words are found on page 14.*

This is a living thing.

Some things are **nonliving things**.

Nonliving things cannot eat or **drink**.

Living things eat and drink.

Nonliving things cannot **breathe**.

Living things breathe.

Nonliving things cannot **grow**.

Living things grow.

Nonliving things cannot have **babies**.

Living things have babies.

Nonliving things cannot **move** on their own.

Living things move on their own.

Word List
Sight Words

are

cannot

eat

have

on

or

own

some

their

Words to Know

babies

breathe

drink

grow

move

nonliving things

31 Words

Some things are **nonliving things**.

Nonliving things cannot eat or **drink**.

Nonliving things cannot **breathe**.

Nonliving things cannot **grow**.

Nonliving things cannot have **babies**.

Nonliving things cannot **move** on their own.

NONLIVING THING

Written by: Kim Thompson
Designed by: Rhea Wallace
Series Development: James Earley
Proofreader: Kathy Middleton
Educational Consultant: Marie Lemke M.Ed.

Photographs:
Shutterstock: Rusian Ivantsov: cover; Valentina Proskurina: p. 1; artpage: p. 3; donnygevie: p. 3b; Maraze: p. 4; VladimirYa: p. 5; Rollingrock: p. 7; Daris Bastet Felis: p. 7b: Vasiliy Budarin: p. 9; 68inches of pleasure: p. 9b; Tatjana Wagner: p. 10; Evelyn D. Harrison: p. 11; Karelnoppe: p. 12; Tatyaby: p. 13

Crabtree Publishing

crabtreebooks.com   800-387-7650
Copyright © 2024 Crabtree Publishing

Printed in the U.S.A./072023/CG20230214

Published in Canada
Crabtree Publishing
616 Welland Ave.
St. Catharines, Ontario
L2M 5V6

Published in the United States
Crabtree Publishing
347 Fifth Ave
Suite 1402-145
New York, NY 10016

Library and Archives Canada Cataloguing in Publication
Available at Library and Archives Canada

Library of Congress Cataloging-in-Publication Data
Available at the Library of Congress

Hardcover: 978-1-0398-0967-3
Paperback: 978-1-0398-1020-4
Ebook (pdf): 978-1-0398-1126-3
Epub: 978-1-0398-1073-0